WORKING TOGETHER ALONE

The Beauty and Freedom of Outsourcing

DORINE RIVERS
PhD, PMP

ALPHA **81** INC.

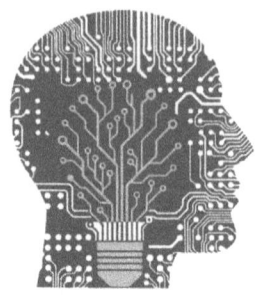

First Edition

Rivers, Dorine. Working Together Alone written by
Dorine Rivers
Library of Congress Control Number 2023908932
ISBN: 979-8-9883658-0-8
Non-Fiction/Business

www.WorkingTogetherAlone.com
www.BrainToBank.com

Published by Alpha 81 Inc.
DBA Alpha 81 Publishing
Carefree, Arizona

WORKING
TOGETHER
ALONE

The Beauty and Freedom
of Outsourcing

DORINE RIVERS, PhD, PMP
INTERNATIONAL BEST SELLING AUTHOR

This book is dedicated to
business owners, managers of humans and non-humans,
and action-oriented entrepreneurs
who have the guts to dare mighty things and
get out there and make things happen!

"If you really want to grow as an entrepreneur, you've got to learn to delegate."

~ *Richard Branson, British entrepreneur*

CONTENTS

CHAPTER 1
SOLOSOCIALIZING

"The best executive is the one who has sense enough to pick good men to do what he wants done, and self restraint enough to keep from meddling while they do it."
~ Theodore Roosevelt, 26th U.S. President

One day I sat in Starbucks absentmindedly sipping my reg Flat White Grande with one hand and clicking away on my laptop with the other while glancing around at the room packed with similar solos doing the same thing. Most of them were wearing headsets and obviously ignoring... or wanting to ignore... all that was around them.

I fit right in. I had come here to work and to solosocialize... ignore everyone around me while feeling I was part of a group and immersed in the company of others.

Solosocializing is what we do when we go to a crowded place to be alone. Most of us have no intention of talking or engaging with anyone there except to place our coffee (or tea) order:
"

I'll have a quad long-shot Grande in a Venti cup, half-caf double cupped no sleeve, salted caramel mocha latte with 2 pumps of sugar-free vanilla but if you don't have sugar-free then no vanilla but then add two extra pumps of white mocha, made with soy at 120 degrees and a java chip inclusion with whipped cream. Please."

We don't wait in the pick-up line to grab our order the minute it's up because we might get stuck talking to someone we don't know, so we hustle back to our table. Mindlessly, we lamely begin the task of getting our products from mind to market while listening for our names to be called.

We like being there by ourselves. It gives us the freedom to get stuff done without interference, yet we're not completely alone.

Being a one-person business, a.k.a. solopreneur, is much the same. We like being the creator of our new product. We like doing it our way and making the decisions, whether good or not-so-good, and we relish the ability to bring on other contributors when and how needed. Alone.

I've been conducting business this way my entire life. It works for me. It will work for you too if working together alone is your preferred modus operandi.

Why Going Solo Is the New Cool

There are days when you spend a lot of time at your coffee/tea hangout of choice. And then there are times when you spend the entire day on the phone, in appointments, and in meetings you'd rather not attend. These are the days you hustle through each event, one after another, eating a half-devoured nutrition bar just to keep going. At the end of the day or night, you're exhausted, a spent mayfly dangling on the end of the line.

Then there are those glorious days when you have an entire "office day." Alone. The only person you talk to is yourself as your mind's self-chatter explodes into a million prismatic wavelengths, energizing you with new ideas, problem-solving eurekas, and excess energy you later need to burn off with a second workout. You talk to no one. Well... maybe you break down and give an occasional shout- out to Siri or Alexa or Google, but mostly... it's just you. You get stuff done. Lots of stuff. Because you can.

However, being a one-person business, a.k.a. solopreneur, doesn't mean you're the only one working in your business. It means you are the core – the center – of all that happens, like the hub of a many-spoked wheel racing down the highway of entrepreneurship. All of the various components that go into creating and maintaining this multi-dimensional wheel are linked to you, but they operate independently as each spoke completes a very specific task or set of tasks.

Few companies, especially start-ups, are able to fulfill all of the needed processes and systems in-house... which usually means doing every one of them yourself.

For example, you know you need to create a website, or at least a landing page, for your new business to promote your product or service. You suck at web design, and you don't want to spend endless hours on web template platforms watching how to "easily" put together your website via WordPress, which is once again something you have to Google several times to figure out.

Like a DC Comics crime victim, you wholeheartedly embrace the idea of a flowing-caped superhero flying to your rescue and completing each dreaded chore.

To the rescue: Outsourcing!

The art of outsourcing includes working with people you know in accounting, graphic design, branding and marketing, video, editing, and endless other niche industries.

It also includes working with people you don't know, such as domestic and global Virtual Assistants (commonly referred to as VAs). Don't worry, you won't need to learn foreign languages or experience culture shock in any way... although you will need to work around various global time zones occasionally.

You will for sure need to fine-tune your communication skills. More on this in a minute.

Here's the coolest part about outsourcing: Subcontracting the areas of business and product development you don't feel completely at home or confident about means you will most likely be working with competent individuals for each of these important tasks. Outsourcing eliminates mistakes one might make while trying to save money by doing things not even a video on YouTube could adequately teach.

Outsourcing is truly the best way to get stuff done if you don't want to wear 50 hats and wonder *when oh when is this going to get easier*?

Hiring remote workers and VAs may seem like an unnecessary expense, especially if you are still trying to get your new company up and running.

But know this: It has been estimated that hiring virtual assistants can save you as much as 40 percent in business expenses. These savings can then be allocated to other areas of your business.

Yeah baby, take that one to the bank!

Outsourcing – Who Not How

When multiple tasks simultaneously arise like swarming bees from an overcrowded hive, the first question we usually ask ourselves is: "HOW will I get all of this done?" The good news is, you now have a new question you'll ask yourself: "WHO can I outsource this to?"

A great read on the art of delegating is the book *Who Not How* by Dan Sullivan and Dr. Benjamin Hardy. The authors state: "Making this shift involves retraining your brain to stop limiting your potential based on what you can do on your own and instead focus on the infinite and endless connections between yourself and other people as well as the limitless transformation possible through those connections."

For more than a decade I consulted for veterinary clinics, creating more efficient and effective processes and systems for their businesses. I quickly learned that veterinarians were used to doing almost everything themselves, including giving vaccinations, changing bandages, and administering medications. What this meant for the bottom line is their time was used up every day doing tasks that could have been given to assistants, kennel attendants, and other workers at the clinic.

The first piece of advice I'd give medical professionals — or any other type of professional — to help their practice become more profitable is this: never do a task you can delegate. Your only tasks and duties are those that require your specific degree, certification, and license to complete.

It is even more critical for entrepreneurs — especially solopreneurs — to outsource everything that does not involve major decisions and the core competencies that are the strategic focus of the business. This maximizes profitability by keeping you, the CEO and backbone of the company, spending time *on* the business, not *in* the business.

If you hire and then manage your outsourced workers correctly, you will reap the benefits of selective delegation in many ways:

- Virtual Assistants are hired on a contractual basis and therefore are easily terminated and replaced if they don't work out.
- Many of the freelancers you hire may be overseas, which means they will get work done while you sleep. Give them your instructions for the next day at the end of your day, and when you wake up, *voilà!* The work is in your inbox.
- You won't need to spend a lot of time training your virtual assistant because you have already chosen a pro who knows how to get the job done. Your ability to communicate a job succinctly and accurately is the key to shortening the amount of time they need to complete it.

Outsourcing - The First Step Toward Growth

As you can see, outsourcing can be one of the best ways to start offloading tasks and work you don't have the bandwidth to complete.

Here's a truth about using unknown freelancers: you may initially have to work through a couple of inexperienced or dishonest hires before you find one that truly fits your niche and needs. Keep in mind that freelancers and contractors come in all shapes, sizes, and skill levels, so you will need to prepare for the possibility that a few may not offer the exact services you seek.

If you are going to grow your business, then you will eventually need to build a team around you and your idea. As an entrepreneur, outsourcing work or specific tasks is a great way to dip your feet into the realm of growth and scaling your business.

If you have been operating as a one-person show so far (a.k.a. solopreneur), this may be the first time you have handed a portion of your project to someone else. Stop and take a deep breath and have faith in the outsourcing system. Nine times out of 10, my freelancers have become committed, passionate partners in my entrepreneurial journey. Why? Because they are small business owners just like me, so they have a vested interest in my success as well as their own. This is one of the many advantages of the aforementioned symbiotic relationship called win/win.

Freelance entrepreneurs are working their tails off just like you to try and bring their own ideas to the market. Their product may be different from yours — graphic design, copywriting, social media content curation — but they are traveling down the same road as you to see their own ideas come to life.

Have I occasionally had a rough experience with freelancers? Yes, I even had to fire a few as they hadn't been honest about their ability to produce the product I had paid for (yes, you usually pay in advance and the money is held in escrow). That's okay because it's still worth the risk. The majority of those offering services have been more than competent to give me what I needed and have saved me large swaths of time I'd have spent first learning how to do it and then doing it. Yes, time is money.

If you see your freelancer or VA as a partner rather than an employee, you will begin to build a managerial presence others will want to follow and support. Treat these workers well and invite them into your process and they will become invaluable partners throughout the rest of your journey.

With any luck, you will begin to build skills and abilities in leading others that will pay off massively in the days ahead. When the moment comes when you are ready to scale your business from solopreneur to enterprise, you will look back on your early days of outsourcing with thankfulness. And most likely, you'll continue to maintain some outsourcing partners on a regular basis, because it will still be an efficient and effective thing to do.

Running a business using online services and collaborators is a great way to get things done and add much-needed resources to your team — whether permanently or just for one project.

Some of the platforms I like and use are listed here: www.BrainToBank.com/Resources.

You don't have to choose one platform... try several, to find the ones that fit your budget and also give you quality outsourced results.

Do delegate. Do outsource. It will preserve your sanity.

And then you can get your own stuff done.
"Delegating work works, provided the one delegating works, too."
~ *Robert Half, HR consulting firm*

CHAPTER 2
WHAT TO OUTSOURCE

"If you don't know what to do with many of the papers piled
on your desk, stick a dozen colleagues' [VAs'] initials
on them and pass them along.
When in doubt, route."
~ Malcolm S. Forbes, businessman

Outsourcing nonessential tasks that have occupied much of your time will free you up to do more "executive-type" work such as strategic planning, weighing in on marketing campaigns, and developing tactics for customer relations and retention. You can delegate many nonessentials such as these:

- Phone call coverage
- Email filtering
- Calendar management
- Appointment setting
- Customer Relationship Management (CRM) updates
- Social media management
- Payroll preparation
- Bookkeeping
- Website design and development
- Search Engine Optimization (SEO)
- Content management services
- Digital marketing
- Blogging

- Software development
- Medical, legal, and audio transcription
- Translation services
- Inventory management
- Data protection and security
- Market research

This is the short list. Even though you most likely have the skills to do all or most of these tasks, you won't have the time if you are truly focused on profit-generating activities.

Great Communication is Vital

The key to working with remote teammates is communication. Poor communication will crash your project faster than your mother walking in on a "my parents are away on vacation" teenage party. Communication is the key to getting what you want, how you want it, and when you want it.

Great, not good, communication allows you to streamline processes, gaining efficiency and effectiveness with better results, on time and in budget. In short, communication can either make or break getting your project to market in a timely manner, so you want to fine-tune your ability to let others know exactly what you need and expect. If they don't understand, that's on you.

Communication is even more important when you are not working in a face-to-face environment, but virtually. Without clear, concise, and detailed communication telling employees what you want by when and how, you are wasting time and money, not to mention the headaches you'll get from banging your head against the wall in frustration. The "lost in translation" factor alone is enough to make you want to go back to your paper route, when things were easy and a nap would make up for having to get up at 4:00 am.

To successfully utilize online and remote virtual assistants, you must at all times be able to communicate effectively, or you will not get the results you are expecting. Then you'll have to start over, as in a demoralizing game of *Chutes and Ladders* where you move forward a little bit at a time, only to find yourself suddenly falling down a chute and having to start the climb over. Time waster, money flusher, efficiency killer.

The first thing to do is make sure your freelancer has English skills. The problem with many virtual assistants offering their services is that they list themselves as native English speakers, though they may or may not be.

Sometimes a resume's language skills category will use the grouping *Native or Bilingual*, so that's a possible explanation. Otherwise, you may need to do further investigation.

When outsourcing to a freelancer I've never worked with before, I will research sellers who have successfully completed multiple contracts and gained high ratings. Typically, I use the "Contact Seller" button to check the level of their language expertise. You can email a message to sellers you are considering, asking a few questions, and see how they reply. Even in a short sentence, you can usually tell how well-honed their language skills are.

If they respond to a complex question with just two to four words, they could be avoiding long discussions, and you should most likely pass.

There are also users of Google Translate, who will usually in the end frustrate and ultimately disappoint you. Their skills are most likely self-listed as Basic, or worse, Unspecified.
   Look for the individuals who are:
- Conversational
- Fluent
- Native or Bilingual

I have had good luck with English speakers who are conversational when the project is graphic design, video, or otherwise an arts-related project. But I would not choose a freelancer claiming basic or conversational command of English for tasks involving text or copywriting or editing.

You can always choose a freelancer who is from the U.S. or United Kingdom, but it is not always necessary. Their rates are usually much higher, and for a start-up with limited funds and a tight budget every dollar counts. Still, you can use filters to help you "up" the chance of getting a person with great English skills if you are needing writing, editing, or anything else requiring linguistic expertise.

Things to include in your communication to your freelancer:

1. **Scope** - for example: *Hi Ibrahim: I hope you are doing well! I'm getting ready to record about 20 videos in Camtasia for a training project. If I record them with a green screen background, can you drop in a different background on each one? Each video will be 7 minutes or less. Please let me know if you can do this and time and cost. Thanks!*

2. **Time** - the due date. The major online freelancer portals have a built-in day and time where you can always see when the project is due. There are penalties for sellers who miss the deadline, so no need to micro-manage them daily, as they are already motivated to avoid negative points on their record. Watch out for workers who have procrastinated and in the last hour of the last day want you to extend the deadline so they are not penalized by the platform. Make it very clear when you hire them that you will not extend the deadline and when the project is due it really is due. Mark this date on your calendar so you can make sure the due date target is hit on time.

3. **Cost** – your budget. You will know the cost of the project if it is a flat-rate pricing structure before the freelancer even starts because your money to pay him or her (not including fees or a tip) will be held

in escrow by the company. For example, if I order a gig on Fiverr for graphic design, I know what the seller is charging me... let's say it's $35, plus Fiverr will charge me a flat service fee. This sum is what you will pay in advance to Fiverr. They in turn will release the money to the freelancer if and only if you approve the final delivery.

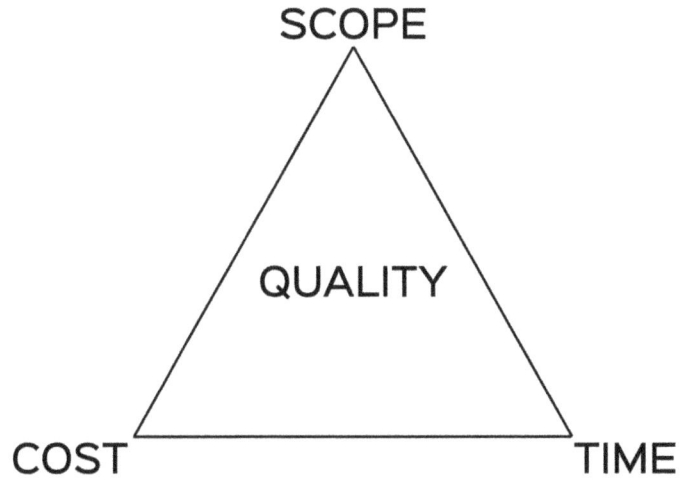

In my initial communication with a seller, I always add detailed bullet points of what I need them to do. I have my expectations in writing before I ever order and pay for the work, in case I need that info later to compare it with the final delivery.

When you order your gig, you will have the opportunity to reiterate what you have already agreed upon. I include my initial communication plus any files in the follow-up request for project details. This triggers the freelancer to begin the project.

When hiring someone you've never worked with, keep the first project you give to them a small one. Don't hire a new virtual assistant and dump 40 hours' worth of work on him/her just because you feel compelled to get all that strangling and stressful stuff off your own plate. Take it slow with a newbie. Test whether this hire is a good fit for you, is efficient and effective, and someone you want to work with regularly.

CHAPTER 3

SEARCHING THE GLOBE FOR VIRTUAL ASSISTANTS

"Hire people who are better than you are, then leave them
to get on with it . . .Look for people who will aim for the
remarkable, who will not settle for the routine."
~ *David Ogilvy, advertising executive*

Where do you find the best virtual assistants, and how do you hire them effectively? Here's some practical advice and tips on where and how you can find the best virtual assistants:

1. **Reputable Websites and Platforms**
   There are many reputable websites and platforms where you can find virtual assistants with various skills. Some of the most popular ones include Upwork, Fiverr, Freelancer.com, and LinkedIn. These platforms allow you to post job listings, browse profiles of potential candidates, and communicate with them directly. You can see a more detailed list here: www.BraintoBank.com/Resources.

2. **Social Media**
   Social media is another great place to find skilled and experienced virtual assistants. LinkedIn and Facebook groups are particularly useful for finding candidates with the specific skills and expertise

you require. You can also search for hashtags related to virtual assistants and remote work to find potential candidates.

3. Referrals

Ask your colleagues, friends, and family for any referrals. They may just know someone with experience in the specific area you're looking for, plus they can also provide valuable insights into the candidate's work ethic and reliability.

4. Job Listings

Post a job listing on your website, social media, or job boards. Be specific about the job requirements and expectations and include information about the specific skills and experience you're looking for. This will help you attract the perfect candidates.

5. Freelance Agencies

Consider working with a freelance agency that specializes in matching virtual assistants with clients. These agencies can save you time and effort since they take care of the screening and vetting process for you.

Once you have found a good number of potential candidates, it's important to interview and select them effectively and carefully. You can do this in a number of ways. Conduct phone or video interviews, request work samples, and ask for references. Establish clear communication, set expectations with your VA, and use project management tools to keep track of their work.

To build a successful long-term relationship with your virtual assistant, you must provide them with regular and consistent feedback and recognize their contributions to your business. By doing this, you're helping to build trust and loyalty, which ensures you get the best results from their work.

Hiring Remote Workers and Virtual Assistants

To hire a virtual assistant, here's the way it usually proceeds on Fiverr:

You contact the seller before you place your order. You want to make sure they can do what you need with expertise and deliver on time. As an example, here's how I communicate with a seller I have used for years. He's my video editing guy based overseas:

Me Jun 25, 12:31 PM

Hi Ibrahim:

I hope you're doing great! I need some minor video editing on 30 short video modules. I need to take the logo off the back end so a company can white label the series. Can you do this for me? If so, by when?

Ibrahim Jun 25, 2:11 PM

Hi River, thanks for contacting me again, yes, I can help you to remove the logo, let me know your budget for all 30 videos, then I will send the offer, and let's start.

Me Jun 25, 2:27 PM

I don't have an idea of cost. Please suggest. It is a simple deletion at the end.

Note: It's better to get the seller to tell you a price first; then you have an idea of how to negotiate.

Ibrahim Jun 25, 2:29 PM

yes, I see, $40 is okay ?

Me Jun 25, 2:30 PM

For all 30 videos?

Ibrahim Jun 25, 2:32 PM

yes all videos.

Me Jun 25, 7:27 PM

Yes, okay. Please send custom order. Thx.

For the next step, you will place your order when the custom offer is sent. Here is an example of what this looks like:

Here's your Custom Offer
$40
I will do professional video editing within 48 hours

Your Offer includes 2-Day Delivery

You will pay before your freelancer starts the work. There are the seller's fees plus the platform fee. For example, this order breaks down as follows:

Professional video editing within 48 hours
2 days $40
SUBTOTAL $40
SERVICE FEE $2 (platform service fee)
TOTAL $42

At this point, you submit your final requirements. This includes any other details you need to communicate as well as files and links such as a Dropbox or Google Docs folder.

Me

Thanks, Ibrahim. Please make sure to complete this in 2 days. Let me know if you have any questions.

Thanks, River.
Next steps:
Your order starts:
Your order started *Jun 26, 08:56 AM*
Your delivery date was updated to June 28 *Jun 26, 08:56 AM*

Then your order is complete.

Ibrahim Jun 28, 08:52 AM

Hello River,

Here are all videos, check it out.

www.drive.google.com/drive

Feel free to ask to edit it further, as you need.

If the video is okay, please mark the order as completed and support me with review.

Thanks, and have a great day! :) Ibrahim

At this point you review the work and make sure it is what you asked for, and if not, you don't accept the delivery, you ask for revisions.

Communication is vital in getting the details of your project completed the way you envisioned. I take a screenshot and mark it up to help clarify what is not correct. Fiverr has a built-in view and mark system that works great, so you can do this right on the platform if you want.

After you get your delivery just the way you want, you accept it. Then you leave a review of their work. You will rate up to 5 stars for each of the following:
- Overall rating
- Communication with seller
- Service as described
- Buy again or recommend
- Leave a tip if you think they earned it

★ ★ ★ ★ ★ Overall rating	*Jun 28, 11:19 AM*
★ ★ ★ ★ ★ Communication with Seller	**Paid with Credit Card**
★ ★ ★ ★ ★ Service as Described	**Tip $8**
★ ★ ★ ★ ★ Buy Again or Recommend	**SUBTOTAL $8**
★ ★ ★ ★ ★ Leave a tip if you think they earned it.	**SERVICE FEE $2**
	TOTAL $10

Note: *For Sellers who do a great job I always leave a tip (at least 20%) and a glowing 5-star review. I tell them what a great job they did, what they did that was exceptional, and that I intend to use them again. And then I do. This does two things: (1) It makes them feel good about their work and working with me; (2) They are eager to work with me again and will put my order ahead of others to please me next time I contact them.*

To break down the effectiveness and efficiency of using this seller, in two days I received 30 edited videos for a total of $62.00 or $2.06 for each video. It was a sweet deal.

Now I could have gone into a software program on my computer and tried to figure out how to do this myself and save the $62.00, but it would have taken me days to learn how to do it and then who knows how this would have turned out, as I am not a professional in video work. Additionally, I was able to use those two days to do other things only I can do, things I cannot farm out to anyone else.

This is the beauty of leveraging your virtual assistants to save you time, money, and most often frustration. Most importantly, you are getting the work done by true professionals, so the output and results of the work exceed the sum of the parts. Brilliant, right?

Cultivate your relationships with those who deliver great work on time and within budget. Hang on to these reliable individuals and companies, as they are hard to find, but once you do, they will work hard and fast for you.

CHAPTER 4

HOW TO USE LINKEDIN TO FIND YOUR DREAM VA

"Leadership is the art of getting someone else to do something you want done because he wants to do it."
~ Dwight Eisenhower, 34th U.S. President

Another very important tool, which is essential to begin your journey of finding your dream VA(s), is LinkedIn. With over 700 million users, LinkedIn is the world's largest professional network and an excellent resource for finding top talent.

LinkedIn's messaging and networking features make it easy to connect with potential VAs and evaluate their suitability for the role. You can review their profiles, work history, and recommendations from previous clients and even initiate a conversation with them to ask questions that help you decide if they are a great fit.

For even more detailed criteria that will save you time and effort in finding your perfect VA(s), I'll show you how to search by:
- Location
- Skills
- Experience

Here's where to start:

1. **Begin by creating a detailed job description via the "WORK" icon.**

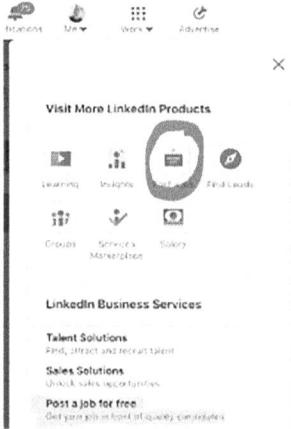

2. **Create a comprehensive and clear job description.**
A good job description should include information about the specific skills and experiences you're looking for in a VA.

Remember: think about your needs in terms of requirements and qualifications. Write them down, as you will end up relaying this information to potential candidates.

Be sure to include keywords related to the type of VA you need; you'll find that this will come in handy when searching for potential candidates. If you look at the box below, you'll see you can add skills after the job description.

← 1 of 2: Job Details

Add a job description

Description *

B *I* U ⊞ ⊞

Add skills

Add skill keywords to make your job more visible to the right candidates (Select up to 10)

(Add skill +)

Take care to be completely clear and include any important details when you write down what you need; otherwise, you'll be bombarded by the wrong profiles, resulting in a huge amount of time reading potentials you will immediately scrap.

Adding skills will help you narrow your search and ensure you only connect with candidates who meet your criteria.

Remember to also add details about what you expect from your VA, including time zone(s) preferred, countries preferred, and any language preferences.

Good communication is key to starting a successful business relationship, so convey your instructions carefully. You want to be as clear as possible. Also, you want to be succinct, yet detailed, so as to leave little room for misinterpretation. Pretend you're a Hollywood screenwriter and that every word on the page counts; otherwise, your actors won't know what to do.

3. **Once you have your job description ready, it's time to search for VAs.**
   LinkedIn has a powerful search function that allows you to narrow your results by location, industry, and other specifics. You can also use keywords related to the job position in your search query for more precise results.

For example, if you are looking for a VA in the Philippines, you can try using keywords like "virtual assistant," "personal assistant," and "administrative support."

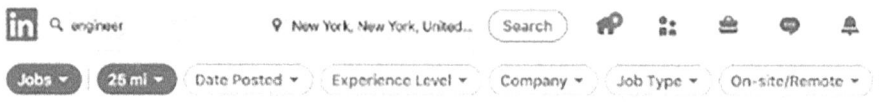

Now it's time to review the profiles, keeping in mind that you need someone with solid communication skills and who knows how to work independently and with little supervision.

4. **When it comes to vetting potential candidates, LinkedIn is an invaluable tool.**
   By using LinkedIn as your VA search platform, you'll receive resumes, cover letters, and the chance to review every candidate's LinkedIn profile. It's very helpful to look at each LinkedIn profile, then go straight to the candidate's previous client or employer recommendations.

   Also, it's critical to look at their portfolio. Why? Because You need to figure out if it's a real or fake portfolio. Yes, even on the best business platform for entrepreneurs and business-minded individuals and companies, not everything is as it appears.

   What to look for: a real portfolio should have tangible evidence of work completed, such as screenshots, links to live websites or social media pages, or detailed case studies. The portfolio should also demonstrate a range of skills and experiences that align with your needs.

   Be wary of portfolios that only contain generic, unbranded samples or those filled with stock images. Additionally, it's important to verify the authenticity of the portfolio by asking for references or conducting a skills test to ensure the virtual assistant is qualified and capable of delivering quality work.

Taking the time to review a virtual assistant's portfolio thoroughly can help you make a well-informed decision and avoid potential scams.

If you're not 100% sure if a portfolio is the real deal or not, you can ask candidates for work samples or to complete a writing test. It's up to you to ask for a trial work period — either paid or done for free — to understand whether the candidate is a good fit for your company right from the beginning.

Below, you can find some practical trials or tests you can ask your future VA to complete:

1. Task-Based Trial: As an example, if you're hiring a virtual assistant for social media management, you can ask them to create a sample social media post for a specific platform like Instagram or Facebook.

   Write down your guidelines and specifications, such as the type of content, style, tone, hashtags, and visuals to use. This will give you an idea of their ability to create effective and engaging social media content.

2. Skill Test: If you're hiring a virtual assistant for graphic design, you can ask them to take a skills test that includes tasks such as creating a logo, designing a banner or flyer, or editing a photo.

   Give them a list of tools and software to use and a timeframe to complete the tasks. This will help you assess their technical skills and proficiency in graphic design.

3. Sample Project: If you're hiring a virtual assistant for content writing, you can ask them to create a sample blog post or article on a topic related to your business. It's important to provide precise guidelines and include things such as word count, tone, and format.

This will give you an idea of their writing style, ability to research and produce quality content, and how well they can adapt to your brand voice.

4. Communication Test: If you're hiring a virtual assistant for customer service, you can set up a mock scenario where you play the role of a client and ask them to respond to a customer complaint via email or chat.

    For the sample project, you should prepare guidelines, such as the type of customer complaint and possible resolutions. This will help you assess their ability to communicate professionally, empathetically, and effectively.

    By conducting a trial, you can assess a virtual assistant's skills and suitability for your business and make a more informed hiring decision.
    And BTW, don't think of paid trials as a waste of resources and money. Once you've narrowed down your three to four final choices, it's important to test them in terms of attitude and skills! It's better to spend a bit to find the right person that you can work with for a long time.

5. **Don't forget the power of networking!**
    References are essential to ensure that a candidate is a good fit for your company. You should avoid hiring a VA with little experience and, therefore, few or no references, as this can be problematic. If they are inexperienced, they may not know how to do their job properly, and you could end up having to train them from scratch once hired, or worse, having to fire them and start all over.

    Remember when you played the childhood game *Mother May I?* and you kept having to take one step forward and two steps backward? Don't do this!

On the other hand, hiring a VA in a junior position could be a good fit, both in terms of salary and experience. If they are willing to learn new things, you can train them in the necessary skills specific to your business. If they are not willing to learn new things, well, there's your answer.

Keep in mind that attitude and personality are essential in a VA. I'd rather choose between someone with a great, optimistic go-getter attitude than someone with massive experience who is a real pain to work with. You can teach skills. You can't teach attitude.

"Your attitude, not your aptitude, will determine your altitude."
~ Zig Ziglar

By following these steps and taking advantage of LinkedIn's powerful search features, you can find your dream VA quickly and easily. With a bit of effort on your part, you'll be well on your way to hiring the perfect VA for your project.

In addition to using LinkedIn to find a virtual assistant, don't forget the plethora of freelance websites previously mentioned. Widen your search to increase your chances of getting the perfect fit by checking out www.BraintoBankcom/Resources.

CHAPTER 5
TIME MANAGEMENT

"The first rule of management is delegation.
Don't try and do everything yourself because you can't."
~ Anthea Turner, British media personality

As a business owner/entrepreneur, time is your most valuable resource. What if a VA could ease your daily schedule and leave you more time to be productive, make more money, or just have fun?! Time management is one of the most important skills a virtual assistant can offer, so why wouldn't you want to take advantage of it?

As you already know, the key to successful time management is to break down tasks into manageable chunks and prioritize them in order of importance. "Chunking" enables you to focus your energy on the tasks with the highest priority while delegating the rest to your VA(s). By delegating tasks to a VA, you can free up your time to center your attention on the high-priority tasks that require your unique skills and expertise... things no one can do but you.

Tasks You Can Delegate RIGHT NOW to a VA

Some examples of tasks you can delegate to a VA to help better manage time and increase productivity are the following:

1. **Email Management**: This is undoubtedly one of the biggest time drains for entrepreneurs; managing email inboxes ranks right up

there with sorting through the garbage looking for recyclables. A virtual assistant can be helpful by filtering out spam, responding to routine emails, and flagging important messages that require your immediate attention. Save your sanity by outsourcing this one first!

2. **Scheduling**: Coordinating meetings and appointments can be a hassle when you're busy enough as it is, so remember a virtual assistant can take care of this for you. A VA can send out invitations, confirm appointments, and even reschedule for you if something urgent comes up.

3. **Social Media Management**: Over the past decade, social media has become an increasingly powerful tool for businesses; it can, however, also be extremely time-consuming. A virtual assistant can handle social media tasks such as scheduling posts, responding to messages, engaging with potential clients and your audience, and monitoring your analytics. Here's a "thumbs up 'like' " for delegating this one!

4. **Data Entry**: You likely already know this, but inputting data can be tedious and time-consuming. If you have YouTube blaring on another computer screen and a bottle of aspirin next to your keyboard, you are likely doing waaaaaaay too much of this activity. But being the quick learner that you are, you've already hired a virtual assistant who can handle data entry tasks such as inputting customer information, tracking expenses, and updating spreadsheets.

5. **Research**: Conducting research can be a prolonged process, but this is one of those essential tasks for businesses that you'll be glad you invested in. Hiring a virtual assistant to do research can include market research, competitor analysis, or product research. You can choose the perfect VA for each project so you get an expert to relay to you things you didn't know you needed to know. Yeah, this one is a vital eye-opener, especially when it comes to researching client avatars, best prices on materials and manufacturing, logistics cost comparison, and the competition.

6. **Bookkeeping**: Keeping track of finances is critical for any business, but it can be overwhelming. You can hire a virtual assistant to handle your bookkeeping tasks, such as invoicing, tracking expenses, and reconciling bank statements. Put your money where your money is and outsource this one. You'll save in the long run.

7. **Travel Arrangements**: We all know that travel planning can be a headache, especially if you're travelling frequently. A VA can handle booking flights, hotels, and rental cars, and even creating itineraries for you. Oh, and your VA can make sure you use, not lose, your travel points before they expire!

There are many additional time management techniques you can work on together with your VA to help you become more productive. Here are some tips that will help:

- Look at your schedule and see where you can cut down on time, especially meetings.
- Write down all tasks that must be completed each day, then prioritize them based on importance and urgency.
- Break down large projects into smaller ones, making them easier to manage and delegate.

Hiring a VA to assist you in your day-to-day business operations means you can ultimately achieve your business goals faster and more efficiently than you would, had you done everything by yourself. Plus, you'll get to have the peace of mind of knowing these routine tasks are being handled efficiently and effectively, leaving you to work ON the business, not IN the business.

So, you see virtual assistants have superpowers! Sans cloaks and swords, their super abilities can free up your time to focus on higher-priority tasks requiring your unique skills and expertise... things no one else can do but you. You get to live more on Maslow's Level 5 – self-actualization – and leave the lower levels to outsourcing.

CHAPTER 6
PROS AND CONS OF HIRING GLOBAL TALENT

"If you pick the right people and give them the opportunity to spread their wings – and put compensation as a carrier behind it – you almost don't have to manage them."
~ *Jack Welch, former CEO at General Electric*

Hiring a Virtual Assistant (VA) from anywhere in the world opens up a plethora of possibilities. The biggest bonus is that it allows you to access global talent and therefore widen the possibilities of getting the best of the best to work for you. For example, you can hire someone with specialized skills and experience that may not be available in your local area, and often at a fraction of the cost, someone who is also extremely good at what they do.

Let's explore both the perks and drawbacks of hiring global talent:

PROS
1. Access to a larger talent pool
When you're limited to hiring locally, you're limited to the talent pool in your area. This means you may be unable to find someone with the specific skills and experience you need. By hiring a VA from basically anywhere in the world, you'll get access to a much larger talent pool, ultimately increasing your chances of finding the perfect fit for your specific business needs. You can

use them for one project, or many, depending on your needs. I have outsourced many projects and many aspects of a project to many regions of the world. I have had outsourcing partners from Russia, Ukraine, Kazakhstan, Morocco, Poland, India, Pakistan, Ireland, Dubai, UK, the USA, and many other countries, some for more than a decade. They are great at what they do and have become valuable team players.

2. **Diverse skill sets**
   Hiring global talent also means you can access someone with a more diverse set of skills. For example, suppose you're based in the United States and need someone to manage your social media accounts. In that case, you may find someone specializing in social media marketing in India or the Philippines. This diversity of skills can actually give you an edge over your competition in the long run as they bring a new way of thinking and usually diverse experience as well.

3. **Cost savings**
   When you hire a VA from a country where the cost of living is lower, you can save money while still getting excellent high-quality work. For example, if you're based in the United States and hire a VA from the Philippines, you can expect to pay a lower hourly rate than you would for someone in the United States. This can mean significant cost savings that can be used elsewhere in your business.

4. **24/7 availability**
   Hiring a VA from a different time zone gives you the benefit of 24/7 availability. Because they're not in your time zone, they can work while you sleep, ensuring your business is always moving forward. This can be especially helpful for businesses with clients or customers in different time zones, including other countries.

5. Increased innovation

When you've got a team from different parts of the world, you have access to a wider range of perspectives and ideas. This can lead to increased innovation and creativity in your business. With a global talent team, you can expect to see fresh ideas and unique approaches to problem-solving, things you never thought of.

6. Cultural awareness

Keep in mind that when you hire global talent, you're also hiring people with different cultural backgrounds and experiences. This can bring a new level of cultural awareness to your business, which can be especially helpful if you've got clients or customers from different parts of the world. This can also help you avoid cultural missteps and makes your business more appealing to a broader range of people.

While hiring global talent has many benefits, you must also consider the potential downsides. Let's explore some of the cons of hiring global talent:

CONS

1. Communication barriers

This is one of the biggest challenges of working with global talent and can include differences in language, cultural norms, and time zones. It can be difficult to establish effective communication and collaboration when working with someone who speaks a different language. Or worse, is in a different time zone and it's ten o'clock at your house and you're tired and want to go to bed and the *ping! ping! ping!* of the app is flooding you with questions from a VA who just got to work. If you don't answer them *now*, then it might cost you a day's work not competed by your VA because they are stuck; they need answers to continue their work. What to do: delegate the VA and his/her questions to someone who handles the VAs!

2. **Different work ethics**

Different cultures have different work ethics, which can possibly create conflicts when working with global talent. For example, in some cultures, taking long breaks during the day is customary, while in others, the workday is expected to be continuous. These differences can lead to misunderstandings and conflicts, and even missed deadlines, which can become quite challenging to navigate.

3. **Legal and tax issues**

You must always be aware of legal and tax issues when hiring global talent. Different countries have different laws and regulations regarding employment, and it can take time to understand these requirements. In most cases, the freelance platform handles these issues. For instance, Fiverr will charge VAT on fees from the total purchase amount when applicable. Here's an example: if Fiverr charges a fee of 10% on a purchase of $100, the VAT (**Value**

Added Tax, or VAT, in the European Union is a general, broadly based consumption tax assessed on the value added to goods and services) is taken from the $10 only, not the entire purchase of $100. Now the required VAT is paid. Appliable U.S. taxes are also charged so you don't have to worry about this requirement. But you must always check specific tax laws to make sure you are in compliance or suffer the consequences of unpaid taxes ruining your newly increased profit margin.

4. **Security concerns**

When working with global talent, you need to be aware of security concerns. This can include issues such as data security and intellectual property protection. When working with someone from a different country, it can be challenging to protect your confidential information and intellectual property. Therefore, you must consider any potential security concerns. It is helpful to hire different VAs for different parts of a large project, so no one VA has all of the information or IP elements. As stated in the book *Brain to Bank,* "Always get legal advice." No, Googling your questions and getting internet answers doesn't count. Think: breathing, living human being. Smart human being. Law school human being.

5. **Cultural differences**

Cultural differences can also create challenges when working with global talent. For example, it's customary in some cultures to address people by their first name, while in others, it's more formal to use their last name. These differences can create misunderstandings and impact the working relationship. In the beginning, you might want to ask questions like: What is your preferred name? Do you prefer written or spoken communication? How do you prefer to receive feedback? What did you eat for breakfast? Just kidding about this last one!

6. **Quality control**

When working with global talent, it can be challenging to ensure complete quality control. It can be difficult to monitor someone's work and ensure they're meeting your standards when they're located in a different country.

Plus, you don't usually see the progression of their work until it is delivered… unless you specify you'd like to see is as it progresses. There's a fine line here between keeping control of your project and micro-managing good and talented people. Sometimes the best thing to do is discuss this, and then see how it goes, tweaking the working relationship until you both know how to best work together.

While hiring global talent has many benefits, it's vital to be aware of the potential downsides that may follow. As we've discussed, a myriad of potential challenges can appear when working with global talent. However, you can ensure a positive and productive working relationship with your global team by being aware of these challenges and taking steps to mitigate them.

CHAPTER 7
HOW TO MANAGE VAs IN DIFFERENT TIME ZONES

"Are we limiting our success by not mastering the art of delegation?
.... it's simply a matter of preparation meeting opportunity."
~ Oprah Winfrey, media mogul

As the world becomes increasingly interconnected, entrepreneurs can tap into a vast pool of talented virtual assistants in different corners of the globe not previously available.

The flexibility of virtual work arrangements means it's possible to work with VAs who operate in different time zones, providing 24/7 support for your business operations. With the right approach and tools, working with VAs in different time zones can unlock opportunities for growth and success in your business. It's like getting the advantage of workers putting in overtime but not paying 1.5 - 2x as much for it.

However, managing teams that work across different time zones can also be challenging. When working with VAs in different parts of the world, a significant time difference may make scheduling and communication more difficult. For example, if you're in the United States and your VA is in India, there may be a ten- to twelve-hour time difference.

Communication breakdowns and missed deadlines can occur when working with VAs who are sleeping while you're awake or vice versa. You don't want either of you to end up suffering from sleep deprivation just to write an email or because you forgot to give a task to your VA.

It's essential to have strategies in place to manage time zone differences and ensure effective communication and collaboration among team members. This requires careful planning and coordination.

It's important to establish clear expectations and protocols for communication. Create a time zone chart showing your VA's working hours, so you can schedule meetings and plan deadlines accordingly. It's also helpful to use tools such as a shared calendar or agenda to help everyone stay on the same page, regardless of location.

But how do we manage all of that? Here are some practical examples of how I manage a dozen or more VAs:

1. **Schedule Overlap:**
   Identify the hours both you and your virtual assistant will be available, and schedule a block of time for daily or weekly check-ins or meetings.

   It's vital to communicate in real time and address any urgent issues or questions. You can use tools like **World Time Buddy** or **Google Calenda**r to find the overlapping hours between time zones.

2. **Task Management**:
   Use task management tools like **ClickUp, Asana** or **Trello** to assign tasks, set deadlines, and track progress. This allows VAs to work on tasks at their own pace and in their own time zone without missing deadlines or waiting for feedback.

3. **Communication Tools:**
   Use communication tools like **Slack** or **Microsoft Teams** to facilitate real-time communication and collaboration. These tools allow you to send messages, make calls, and share files, regardless of time zone differences. Of course, you can also use email to communicate, but it may not be as efficient for real-time communication.

4. **Time Zone Awareness:**
   Ensure everyone on the team is aware of their colleagues' and virtual assistants' time zones. Use tools like **World Time Buddy** or **Clockify** to track time zones and avoid scheduling meetings or deadlines during non-working hours.

By implementing these strategies, you can effectively manage time zone differences and ensure effective communication and collaboration among team members, leading to increased productivity and business efficiency.

Your VAs may need support from you at times when you're unavailable because of the time difference. Without organization and planning, this can potentially create delays and impact your projects' success.

Remember to set clear expectations around communication and establish a system for answering questions and resolving issues, even when you're unavailable. This can include using messaging platforms that allow for asynchronous communication, as you read above, setting up specific times for check-ins, or delegating specific tasks to VAs who work during your available hours.

CHAPTER 8
THE LATEST AND GREATEST TECHNOLOGIES

"Technology is nothing. What's important is that you have a faith in people, that they're basically good and smart, and if you give them tools, they'll do wonderful things with them."
~ Steve Jobs

Not only is having access to the latest technology important for yourself, but it's also important for your team, especially if you're utilizing overseas freelancers. Because technology evolves rapidly, businesses may struggle to keep up with the latest tools and trends.

However, the right virtual assistants can provide access to the latest technology and tools, enabling businesses to stay current and competitive. This is especially true if you have tech-savvy remote workers who specialize in this field. Be prepared to learn things you didn't know and can now implement.

Let's explore how VAs can help businesses access the latest technology and tools and how they've helped businesses stay ahead of the curve.

How Virtual Assistants Can Provide Access to the Latest Technology and Tools

Your virtual assistants should be skilled professionals who can help your business access the latest technology and tools and get them integrated into operations. VAs can also provide training and support to ensure businesses and co-workers use these new technologies effectively.

By monitoring industry news and developments, virtual assistants can help businesses stay updated with the latest trends and innovations. They can alert businesses to emerging technology and tools that could be beneficial and help businesses evaluate whether these tools will be a good fit for their operations. They can even create training modules to educate you and your team.

Examples of How Virtual Assistants Have Helped Businesses Stay Up to Date with the Latest Trends and Innovations:

1. **Social Media Management**
   As you know, social media constantly evolves, with new platforms and features being introduced regularly. Virtual assistants can help businesses stay up to date with the latest social media trends and tools. Here's how: A virtual assistant can help a business set up and manage a Facebook account or provide training on how to use Instagram Reels effectively. Meta's native scheduling tool and Later are two of the most common tools VAs use.

2. **E-Commerce Management**
   The e-commerce landscape is also one that is constantly evolving. As is the case with social media, new platforms and tools are also being introduced regularly. A virtual assistant can help your business stay up to date with the latest e-commerce trends and innovations. For example, you could have a virtual assistant set up and manage your Shopify store. You can even have them provide

training on how your business can utilize Shopify or Facebook Shops effectively.

3. **Cybersecurity**
   Cybersecurity threats are constantly evolving; therefore, it's extremely important that businesses stay up to date with the latest threats and tools for protection. Your VA can help your business stay informed about the latest cybersecurity threats and possibly even provide training on how to prevent them. They can also help businesses evaluate and implement cybersecurity tools to protect their data and systems.

   By staying informed about the latest trends and innovations, virtual assistants can help businesses identify new opportunities for growth and long-term success.

   This is a good place to mention the quickly evolving role of Artificial Intelligence (AI) and how your virtual assistants can use it to provide your business with information on ever-evolving technologies.

   By utilizing platforms such as ChatGPT, Artificial Intelligence (AI) can generate research and information for your business on new technologies in several ways:

   Data analysis: AI can analyze large amounts of data from various sources, including social media, industry reports, and customer feedback, to identify emerging trends and new technologies that businesses can adopt.

   Predictive analytics: AI can use predictive analytics to identify patterns and trends in data, allowing businesses to anticipate future changes in technology and adjust their strategies accordingly.

Natural language processing (NLP): AI can use NLP to analyze customer feedback, reviews, and surveys to identify what customers want and need, providing insights into potential new technologies that businesses can develop or invest in.

Recommendation engines: AI-powered recommendation engines can provide businesses with personalized recommendations for new technologies based on their unique needs and preferences.

Competitive analysis: AI can analyze data from competitors to identify new technologies they are using and determine if they are successful. This information can help businesses decide whether to invest in similar technologies or pursue different options.

By leveraging AI, businesses can stay up to date on emerging technologies and trends, making informed decisions about how to incorporate them into their operations to stay competitive in the market.

It goes without saying that bringing on virtual assistants who are adept at AI will accelerate your company's ability to progress at a much quicker rate, keeping you more informed and ahead of the pack.

CHAPTER 9

BEING AN EFFECTIVE LEADER FOR YOUR VA

"Being a leader is not about being in charge.
It's about taking care of those in your charge."
~ Simon Sinek

When it comes to being a leader, it's not just about having authority or power over others. Being a leader is also about taking responsibility for the well-being and growth of those you lead.

This includes leading a virtual team, even a global one, consisting of assistants and freelancers all over the world who, when led with integrity and selflessness, will outdo themselves in output and quality. The sum will exceed the parts. A great leader can inspire this… and more.

A true leader inspires and motivates their team to achieve their goals while providing necessary guidance and support along the way. They lead by example. They demonstrate integrity, humility, and empathy. They build trust. They foster a culture of collaboration and respect.

Being the leader of a global team is a privilege and a responsibility and requires a commitment to continual growth and development for yourself and your team.

It's not enough to hold a leadership position; a leader must earn the respect and trust of those they lead through their actions and words.

As you have already learned, hiring a virtual assistant is a great way to increase productivity and efficiency in your business. However, managing a VA can be a different experience from managing an in-person employee. You must be an effective leader to get the most out of your VA. Let's explore some tips on how to be a great leader for your virtual assistant.

1. **Set Clear Expectations**
    The first step to being an effective leader for your virtual assistant, as noted earlier, is to set clear expectations. This includes outlining the tasks you want them to complete and defining deadlines and the quality standards you expect from them. Without clear expectations, your VA may not know what they need to do or how they should do it. This usually ends badly for everyone involved.

2. **Communicate Effectively**
    Communication is key to building a successful relationship with your virtual assistant. Ensure you're communicating with them regularly and clearly. Provide feedback on tasks they've completed, answer any questions they may have, and check in on how they're progressing. As previously mentioned, you should also establish a communication schedule that works for you and your VA.

3. **Trust Your Virtual Assistant**
    One of the biggest benefits of hiring a virtual assistant is the ability to delegate tasks and free up your time. However, to do this effectively, you must trust your virtual assistant. You should allow them to complete tasks without micromanaging or second-guessing their work. Trust is built over time, so allow your VA to prove themselves.

4. **Provide Feedback**

   Feedback is essential for growth and improvement. Make sure you're providing feedback to your virtual assistant regularly. This includes both positive feedback when they complete tasks well and constructive feedback when improvements are necessary. Feedback helps your VA grow and improve and demonstrates that you truly value their work.

5. **Invest in Their Training and Development**

   Investing in your virtual assistant's training and development can help them hone their skills and become even more valuable to your business. You can provide them access to training resources, offer them opportunities for professional development, and provide them with regular performance reviews. Investing in your virtual assistant's training and development demonstrates that you value their contribution to your business.

By using these outlined tools, you can build a successful relationship with your VA and improve productivity and efficiency in your business.

Just like keeping a not-so-new car running with frequent oil changes and tune-ups, it's easier and cheaper in the long run to hang onto workers you've nurtured along the way than to start over with someone new.

Did I just sound like a marriage counselor? Sorry!!!!!

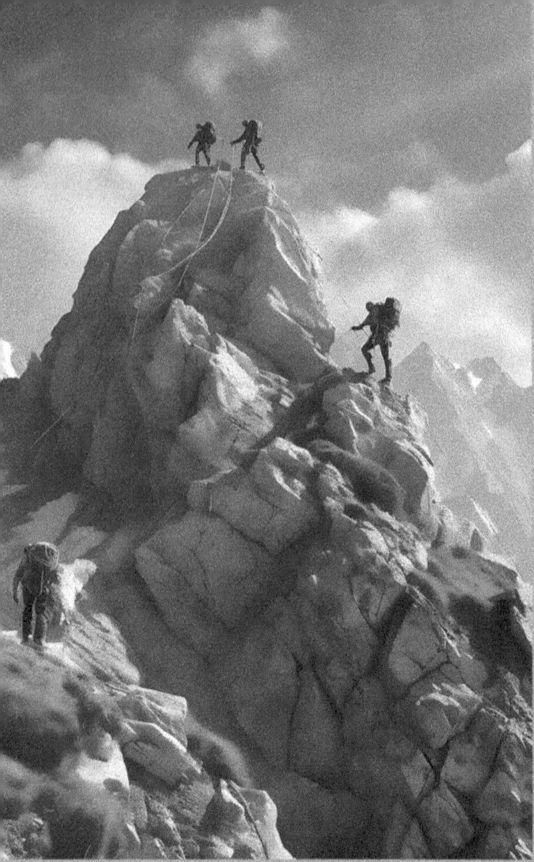
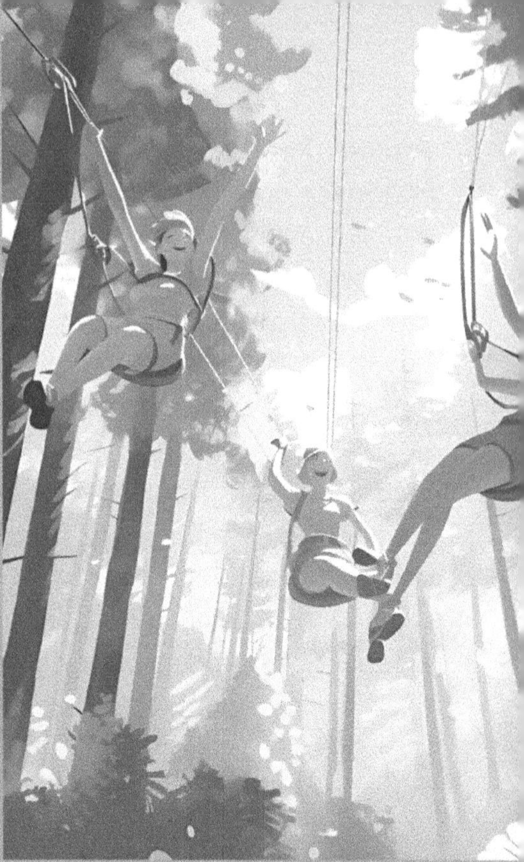
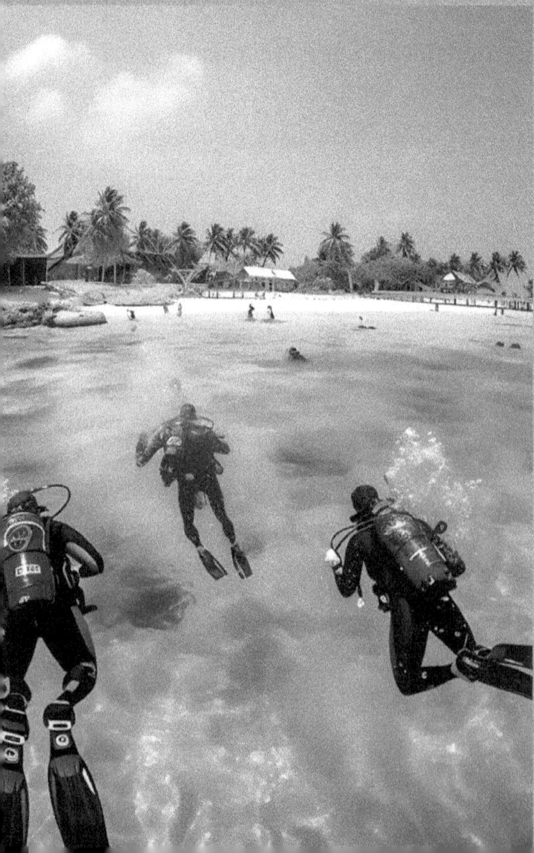
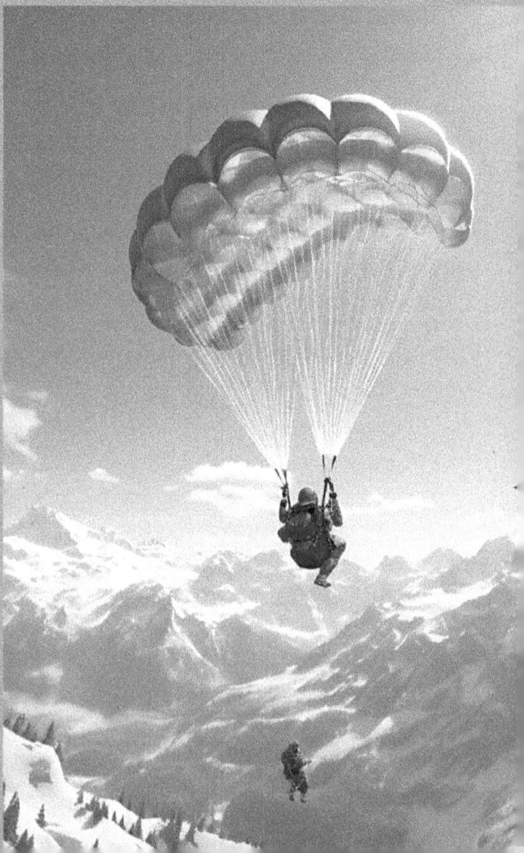

CHAPTER 10
WHAT TO DO WITH YOUR NEWLY FOUND FREE TIME

Think of all the crazy and fun things you could do if you had more of that precious commodity called time.

Many of you reading this book are already making a list in your head which will quickly be converted to paper – a list that includes a zillion new ideas, businesses, and additional projects you will start now that you have your core business under control.

But if you happen to be hitched, betrothed, committed (the good kind, not the white-jacket variety… as in straitjacket), loved, or the BFF of an adventurous and fun type, either they have a super-exotic list, or you will talk them into yours when you come to your senses and decide it's time to LIVE!

If you're short a few… or 100… ideas, here's a list to get you started on what could be your next "I love my VAs because I have more time!" adventure:

A Crazy Lifelong List of the Best 100 Things to Do (because you were smart enough to hire a VA)

1. Volunteer at an elephant rescue in Thailand
2. Sunbathe topless on the French Riviera

3. Dogsled through the Alaskan forest
4. Swim in Jellyfish Lake in Palau
5. Explore the Acropolis in Greece
6. Go gorilla trekking in Uganda/Rwanda
7. Volunteer at an orphanage
8. Cruise on a junk boat through Halong Bay
9. Hike the active Pacaya volcano in Guatemala
10. Take a Christmas Market Cruise through Europe
11. Sleep in an Ice Hotel
12. Get a henna tattoo in India
13. Spend the night in a Tteehouse
14. Hike the Inca Trail to Machu Picchu
15. Stand in front of the Taj Mahal in India
16. See the Changing of the Guard in London
17. Hot air balloon over Cappadocia
18. Hear the Pope speak at the Vatican in Italy
19. Release baby turtles into the ocean
20. Walk the Great Wall of China
21. Make a wish in the Trevi Fountain in Italy
22. Get a fish pedicure
23. Drive Route 66 in the United States
24. Explore the ancient ruins of Petra in Jordan
25. Hike Mt. Nokogiri in the Chiba Prefecture of Japan
26. Dive the Great Barrier Reef
27. Explore the Waitomo Glowworm Cave in New Zealand
28. Give blood
29. Climb Africa's Mount Kilimanjaro
30. Visit Gardens by the Bai in Singapore
31. Castle hop in Ireland
32. Eat at the French Laundry in Napa
33. Run with the bulls in Pamplona in Spain
34. Adopt an animal from a shelter
35. Travel the Trans-Siberian Railway
36. Climb to the peak of Sigiriya Rock in Sri Lanka
37. Drink steins of beer at Oktoberfest in Germany

38. Take a Flyboarding Jetpack flight
39. See an opera at the Sydney Opera House in Australia
40. Attend a music festival
41. Helicopter over a volcano in Hawaii
42. Soak in Pamukkale Hot Springs in Turkey
43. Marvel at Guyana's Kaieteur Falls
44. Sleep in an overwater bungalow in Bora Bora
45. Go to a yoga retreat in Costa Rica
46. Take the Walk of Faith at Tianmen Mountain, China
47. Hike to the top of Bartolome Island in the Galapagos
48. Throw tomatoes at La Tomatina in Spain
49. Swim with whale sharks in Cancun
50. Walk the Spanish El Camino de Santiago de Compostela
51. Experience Istanbul's Call to Prayer at the Blue Mosque
52. Attend the Kentucky Derby
53. Attend Mass at Notre Dame Cathedral in Paris
54. Feed the Swimming Pigs of Exuma
55. Tour a monastery at Meteora in Greece
56. Relax in the Blue Lagoon Hot Springs in Iceland
57. Stay in a Tuscan villa in Italy
58. Go volcano boarding in Nicaragua
59. Be a part of a flash mob
60. Cross the Salarde Uyuni in Bolivia
61. Take a helicopter ride into the Grand Canyon
62. Kayak through icebergs in Greenland
63. Visit all 7 continents
64. Hike between the Towns of Cinque Terre in Italy
65. See the blue-footed booby mating dance in Galapagos
66. Tour the Hanging Temple of Mount Hengshan in China
67. Drink in a Shinjuku Golden Gai Bar in Tokyo
68. Let go of a floating lantern in Taiwan
69. Get spooked at the Catacombs in Paris
70. See the Northern lights
71. Ride in a gondola in Venice
72. Watch the Grand Prix in Monaco

73. Visit a Maasai tribe in Tanzania

74. Attend Burning Man in Nevada

75. Skydive

76. Zip line through the rain forest of Costa Rica

77. Visit all 50 states

78. Trek to Mount Everest Base Camp in Nepal

79. Kayak with beluga whales in Manitoba

80. Attend the Palio Horse Race in Siena

81. Explore the depths of a Cava cave in Spain

82. Drive Maui's Road to Hana

83. Watch wrestling practice at a Sumo Stable in Tokyo

84. Wear a mask at Carnival in Venice

85. Eat at a themed restaurant in Tokyo

86. Go truffle hunting in Tuscany

87. Go on an African Safari

88. Get scrubbed at a Hamam in Turkey

89. Eat insects at Chiang Mai's Sunday Night Market

90. Float in the Dead Sea

91. Hike to the top of Piaynemo in Raja Ampat

92. Visit Dracula's Castle in Transylvania, Romania

93. Eat at the cheapest Michelin-starred restaurant

94. See a Broadway musical in New York City

95. Go Tidal Bore rafting in Nova Scotia

96. Interact with the penguins of Antarctica

97. Explore the Silent City of Mdina in Malta

98. Walk through a rice terrace in Indonesia

99. Have a home stay in Norway with a Sami reindeer herder

100. Participate in a Japanese Tea Ceremony

Used with permission. Thank you Annette White of BucketListJourney.net!

Oh, and send me postcards please! Something like: "Wish you were here" or "Eat your heart out" or "Jealous?"
Send to: River * PO Box 5383 * Carefree, AZ 85377.

CHAPTER 11
WRAPPING IT UP

"If you want to do a few small things right, do them yourself. If you want to do great things and make a big impact, learn to delegate."
~ *John C. Maxwell, American author*

Okay, you've already discovered what it's like to be a business owner, a manager of humans, or the ever-adventurous entrepreneur or you wouldn't be reading this book.

You're here because, to paraphrase Hans and Franz, "You want to pump it up!" Okay then: Let's get better and stronger at what we do!

Here's what you should have learned:
- √ Why going solo is the new cool
- √ How to implement "Who Not How"
- √ Why outsourcing is the first step toward growth
- √ What to outsource
- √ Why communication is vital
- √ How to search the globe for virtual assistants
- √ How to hire remote workers and virtual assistants
- √ How to use LinkedIn to find your dream VA
- √ How to utilize time management to optimize your VAs
- √ What tasks you can delegate right now to a VA
- √ The pros and cons of hiring global talent
- √ How to manage VAs in different time zones

- √ How Virtual Assistants can provide access to the latest technology & tools
- √ How to be an effective leader for your VA
- √ How hiring a virtual assistant helped an entrepreneur scale her business
- √ Now that you have more time: What to choose for your next adventure!

KEY POINT to REMEMBER: Outsourcing tasks shouldn't be daunting. Rather, it should make your life much easier, allowing you to focus on what YOU are good at, like using your skills and unique expertise to do those tasks only YOU can do.

A virtual assistant is an asset who can lower your business costs significantly without compromising your productivity. In fact, your assistants will increase productivity exponentially if you choose and manage them properly.

So... what are you waiting for?

> "What we do today, right now, will have an accumulated effect on all our tomorrows."
> ~ Alexandra Stoddard, Author

It's today. Right now... it's still today.

Turn the page to ACTION ACCELERATORS and advance your newly-acquired knowledge into ACTION.

Chapter 12
ACTION ACCELERATORS

THINK IT ⟶ ORGANIZE IT ⟶ DO IT

Okay, you've been schooled. It's time to do something about it!

Take action on these items NOW!

1. Go to your favorite coffee/tea shop and order the most obnoxious drink you can imagine. Just kidding — but you get extra credit if you really do this.

2. Check out at least three freelancer websites. I recommend one of them to be Fiverr, as it is easily navigable, cheap to play around on, and they are ever progressive in enhancements and advancements.

3. Choose at least three things you need to or will outsource to make your life easier. Choose from the following list or create three of your own items:
   - Phone call coverage

- Email filtering
- Calendar management
- Appointment setting
- CRM updates
- Social media management
- Bill paying and payroll preparation
- Bookkeeping
- Website design and development
- SEO
- Content management services
- Digital marketing
- Blogging
- Software development
- Medical, legal, and audio transcription
- Translation services
- Inventory management
- Data protection and security
- Market research

4. Hire three different freelancers (it doesn't matter if they are on the same platform) and learn the ropes of communicating and working with them.

5. If you want to learn more about how virtual assistants can help you save time and increase productivity, be sure to check out my new book, *Brain to Bank.* You'll discover even more tips and strategies for leveraging virtual assistants to take your business to the next level. You can buy it today on Amazon: http://amzn.to/3LyCjgO.

6. Enjoy the freedom of freelancers and outsourcing. And please email me and tell me which of the 100 "Now I Have Time" adventures... or another one you've been waiting to explore... you went on! No, really, I can't wait to hear all about it!

   DR@Alpha81.com

7. Now go make things happen!

VIRTUAL ASSISTANTS TRACKING SHEETS

Use these tracking sheets to organize your virtual assistants, various tasks, and keep things moving ahead!

- Bookkeeping/Payroll AND Inventory Management
- Calendar Management AND Scheduling
- Content Management AND Blogs
- Customer Surveys & Feedback AND Customer Relations Management (CRM)
- Digital Marketing AND Presentation Design
- Email Management AND Phone Calls
- Event Promotion AND Travel Arrangements
- Graphic Design AND Video Content Creation
- Media Management AND Data Protection & Security
- Research AND Data Entry
- Social Media Management AND Social Media Advertising
- Transcription Services AND Translation Services
- Website Creation/Maintenance AND Website Analytics (+SEO)

Task: Bookkeeping/Payroll	VA Name	Outsource Platform	Date Hired	Due Date

Task: Inventory Management	VA Name	Outsource Platform	Date Hired	Due Date

Task: Calendar Management	VA Name	Outsource Platform	Date Hired	Due Date

Task: Scheduling	VA Name	Outsource Platform	Date Hired	Due Date

Task: Content Management	VA Name	Outsource Platform	Date Hired	Due Date

Task: Blogs	VA Name	Outsource Platform	Date Hired	Due Date

Task: Customer Surveys & Feedback	VA Name	Outsource Platform	Date Hired	Due Date

Task:Customer Relations Management (CRM)	VA Name	Outsource Platform	Date Hired	Due Date

Task: Digital Marketing	VA Name	Outsource Platform	Date Hired	Due Date

Task: Presentation Design	VA Name	Outsource Platform	Date Hired	Due Date

Task: Email Management	VA Name	Outsource Platform	Date Hired	Due Date

Task: Phone Calls	VA Name	Outsource Platform	Date Hired	Due Date

Task: Event Promotion	VA Name	Outsource Platform	Date Hired	Due Date

Task: Travel Arrangements	VA Name	Outsource Platform	Date Hired	Due Date

Task: Graphic Design	VA Name	Outsource Platform	Date Hired	Due Date

Task: Video Content Creation	VA Name	Outsource Platform	Date Hired	Due Date

Task: Media Management	VA Name	Outsource Platform	Date Hired	Due Date

Task: Data Protection & Security	VA Name	Outsource Platform	Date Hired	Due Date

Task: Research	VA Name	Outsource Platform	Date Hired	Due Date

Task: Data Entry	VA Name	Outsource Platform	Date Hired	Due Date

Task: Social Media Management	VA Name	Outsource Platform	Date Hired	Due Date

Task: Social Media Advertising	VA Name	Outsource Platform	Date Hired	Due Date

Task: Transcription Services	VA Name	Outsource Platform	Date Hired	Due Date

Task: Translation Services	VA Name	Outsource Platform	Date Hired	Due Date

Task: Website Creation/ Maintenance	VA Name	Outsource Platform	Date Hired	Due Date

Task: Website Analytics (+SEO)	VA Name	Outsource Platform	Date Hired	Due Date

GLOSSARY

Adventurous
Adventurous describes someone who is eager to take risks, try new experiences, and explore new places or activities. Think outdoors. Think business!

AI (Artificial Intelligence)
AI is a branch of computer science that aims to create machines capable of performing tasks that typically require human intelligence, such as problem-solving, learning, and decision-making.

Asynchronous Communication
Asynchronous communication is any type of communication where one person provides information, and then there is a time lag before the recipients take in the information and offer their responses.

Asset
An asset is something valuable and advantageous to a person or a business. Virtual assistants are considered assets when they contribute to increased productivity and efficiency in a business.

Attitude
Attitude is a person's mindset, outlook, or disposition towards work, challenges, and interactions with others. When hiring a virtual assistant, a positive and optimistic attitude on their part is essential for a successful working relationship.

Blogging
Blogging is writing and publishing articles, posts, or content on a website or a blog. Blogs are a popular way for individuals and businesses to share information, insights, and updates with their audience. Blogs are usually published with some kind of regularity, and written in a friendly, informal way. Great task for a VA!

Brain To Bank
https://www.braintobank.com/resources is a resource on the BrainToBank.com website related to free outsourcing and entrepreneurial resources. Dig in!

Bulleted Points
A list of concise and clear statements presented in bullet form for easy reading and understanding.

Check-ins
Check-ins are regular meetings or updates where team members discuss progress, share information, and address any questions or issues.

Communication
Communication is the exchange of information, ideas, and instructions between individuals or parties. Effective communication with your virtual assistants is vital for clear task delegation, feedback, and collaboration.

Cost of Living
The cost of living refers to the expenses needed to maintain a certain standard of living in a particular location, including housing, food, transportation, and other necessities.

CRM Updates
CRM stands for Customer Relationship Management. CRM updates are the recording and updating of the information and interactions of

a company's customers or clients in a CRM system. This can include adding new customer data, updating contact details, and recording customer interactions.

Cybersecurity
Cybersecurity refers to the protection of computer systems, networks, and data from digital attacks and unauthorized access. It involves implementing measures to prevent and detect security breaches.

Data Analysis
Data analysis is the process of examining and interpreting data to extract useful information, identify patterns, and make informed decisions.

Data Protection and Security
Data protection and security involve safeguarding sensitive information and data from unauthorized access, theft, or damage. This includes implementing measures such as encryption, firewalls, access controls, and regular data backups.

Delegation
Delegation means entrusting or assigning tasks, responsibilities, or authority to someone else. In the context of entrepreneurship, it refers to the process of giving tasks or responsibilities to others, such as virtual assistants, to free up time and enable you to focus on more important aspects of the business so you can do the things only YOU can do.

Digital Marketing
Digital marketing encompasses various online marketing strategies and tactics to promote a business, product, or service. It includes activities such as social media marketing, email marketing, content marketing, search engine marketing, and more.

Diverse Experience

Diverse experience means a wide range of different skills, knowledge, and background. A virtual assistant with diverse experience is versatile, adaptable, and can quickly grasp new concepts or tools required for specific projects. This makes them an asset to entrepreneurs, businesses, and professionals who would like assistance with multiple aspects of their operations without having to hire multiple specialists. It allows clients to delegate a wide range of tasks to a single virtual assistant, streamlining workflow and enhancing productivity.

Drawbacks

Drawbacks, in the context of business, are the disadvantages, limitations, or negative aspects associated with a particular decision, strategy, product, service, or the overall operation of a company. These drawbacks can hinder the growth, profitability, efficiency, or reputation of a company. It is essential for business owners and managers to identify and address drawbacks proactively to minimize their impact on the organization and its success. Some common examples of drawbacks in business include increased costs, decreased productivity, market competition, regulatory compliance challenges, negative customer feedback, and technological limitations.

Email Management

Email management means organizing and handling email communications efficiently. A virtual assistant can assist in filtering and responding to emails, as well as flagging important messages that require immediate attention. A skilled virtual assistant can also draft and send routine responses or follow-up messages on behalf of a client, ensuring timely replies and maintaining professionalism in all email communications. They may create email templates for commonly asked questions or inquiries, streamlining the response process and saving the client valuable time.

Empathy
Empathy is the ability to understand and share the feelings and per-spectives of others. An empathetic leader shows compassion and consideration for their team members' emotions and experiences.

Enterprise
In the context of business, an enterprise refers to a large-scale orga-nization or company, often with multiple employees and operations.

Escrow
In the context of payments, escrow refers to the holding of funds by a third party until certain conditions are met, usually as part of a transaction or contract.

E-commerce Management
E-commerce management involves overseeing and managing the online sales and operations of a business, including setting up and managing online stores, handling product listings, processing orders, and managing customer interactions.

Flash Mob
A flash mob is a group of people who gather in a public place, per-form a brief and unexpected performance or act, and then disperse quickly, often to surprise and entertain bystanders.

Flat-Rate Pricing Structure
A pricing model where a fixed or flat fee is charged for a particular service, regardless of the amount of work or time required.

Fraction of the Cost
An expression you may hear referring to the fact that hiring global talent can often be more cost-effective than hiring locally, resulting in lower expenses.

Freelance Agencies

Freelance agencies are organizations or companies that specialize in matching freelancers, including virtual assistants, with clients who need their services. These agencies handle the screening and vetting process for clients, making it easier for entrepreneurs to find suitable virtual assistants.

Freelancer

A freelancer is a self-employed individual who offers their services to clients on a project or contract basis. Freelancers work independently and may provide various services, such as writing, design, programming, or the performing of administrative tasks.

Fiverr

Fiverr is an online marketplace where freelancers offer their services, known as "gigs," to clients. It is a platform where entrepreneurs can find and hire freelancers for various tasks and projects.

Global Talent

Global talent refers to skilled professionals from many different parts of the world. Hiring global talent allows entrepreneurs to access a diverse pool of skills and experiences beyond their local area.

Humility

Humility is the quality of being humble and modest. A humble leader does not boast or act arrogantly, but instead treats others with respect and acknowledges their strengths and contributions.

Integrity

Integrity means being honest and ethical, having strong moral principles. A leader with integrity acts consistently with their values and principles.

Inventory Management
Inventory management refers to the process of overseeing and controlling a company's inventory or stock of products. It involves tracking inventory levels, monitoring stock movement, and ensuring that products are available when needed.

Japanese Tea Ceremony
The Japanese Tea Ceremony, also known as Chanoyu or Sado, is a traditional cultural activity in Japan that involves the ceremonial preparation and consumption of matcha (powdered green tea). It is a highly ritualistic and meditative practice.

Job Description
A job description is a document that outlines the specific responsibilities, duties, qualifications, and expectations for a particular job or position within an organization. In this context, it refers to the detailed description of the tasks and skills required for a virtual assistant position.

Job Listings
Job listings are advertisements or postings that describe job opportunities and the requirements for candidates. Entrepreneurs can post job listings on their website, social media, or job boards to attract potential virtual assistant candidates.

Keywords
Keywords are words or phrases that are relevant to a specific topic or job position. When crafting a job posting, entrepreneurs should include specific keywords that reflect the key responsibilities, qualifications, and areas of expertise they are looking for in a virtual assistant. These keywords could encompass various aspects, such as administrative skills (e.g., scheduling, data entry, and file management), technical abilities (e.g., proficiency in specific software or

tools), communication skills (e.g., email management and customer support), and industry-specific knowledge (e.g., social media marketing or content creation).

Maasai Tribe
The Maasai tribe is a pastoral ethnic group living in Kenya and Tanzania. They are known for their distinct culture, traditional clothing, and unique way of life, centered around cattle herding.

Managerial Presence
The ability of an entrepreneur or manager to lead and exert influence within their team or organization. Managerial presence goes beyond just having a position of authority; it encompasses a set of qualities and behaviors that command respect, instill confidence, and inspire trust among team members and colleagues. A strong managerial presence is crucial for effective leadership and a positive work environment.

Mark Up
In this context, marking up refers to the act of adding annotations or comments to a document or file to provide feedback or clarification.

Market Research
Market research is the process of gathering and analyzing information about a market, including customers, competitors, and industry trends. It helps businesses make informed decisions and develop effective strategies.

Micro-Managing
Micro-managing is a management style where a person closely observes and controls every small aspect of a project or task, often leading to a lack of autonomy and demotivation of team members.

Networking
Networking involves building relationships and connections with other professionals or individuals in a specific industry or field. In the context of finding a virtual assistant, networking can help entrepreneurs gather references and recommendations for potential candidates.

Newbie
In this context, a newbie refers to a new or inexperienced freelancer or virtual assistant who is starting to work with a particular platform, client, or employer for the first time.

Nonessential Tasks
These are tasks that are not critical to the core operations or profit-generating activities of a business. Outsourcing nonessential tasks allows entrepreneurs to focus on more strategic and important aspects of their business.

Non-Working Hours
Non-working hours refer to the times when individuals are not actively working or available for business-related activities. This varies based on individual schedules and time zones.

Outsourcing
Outsourcing refers to the practice of contracting or delegating tasks and services to external individuals or companies instead of handling them in-house.

Palio Horse Race
The Palio is a traditional horse race held twice a year in Siena, Italy. It is a fiercely competitive event between different neighborhoods (contrade) of the city, with each contrada represented by a horse and jockey.

Performance Review

A performance review is a process in which a leader evaluates an employee's performance, provides feedback, and discusses areas for improvement or development. These are seldom held for virtual assistants but may be considered for long-term freelancers.

Perks

Perks are the benefits or advantages associated with a particular action or decision. In the context of business and employment, perks are additional advantages or special privileges offered to employees or clients beyond their regular compensation or service. Perks are designed to enhance job satisfaction, improve employee morale, attract top talent, and retain valuable team members. They can also be used as incentives to build strong client relationships and foster customer loyalty.

Platform Service Fee

This is the fee charged by a platform, such as Fiverr, for using their services to hire and work with virtual assistants and other freelancers. It is an additional cost on top of the payment to the virtual assistant for their services.

Predictive Analytics

Predictive analytics is the use of data, statistical algorithms, and machine learning techniques to identify patterns and predict future outcomes or trends.

Project Management Tools

Project management tools are software programs or applications that help entrepreneurs and teams organize, track, and collaborate on various tasks and projects. These tools are useful for managing the work of virtual assistants and keeping track of progress and deadlines.

Quality Control

Quality control refers to the process of ensuring that products, services, or work meet the standards and expectations of the business or client. Quality control is an essential aspect of business operations, encompassing a range of activities and procedures aimed at identifying and rectifying any defects, errors, or discrepancies in products, services, or work processes. The primary goal of quality control is to deliver consistent, high-quality outcomes that meet or exceed customer expectations. Effective quality control not only ensures customer satisfaction but also enhances the reputation of the business, increases operational efficiency, reduces waste and rework, and ultimately leads to improved profitability and competitiveness in the marketplace.

Real-Time Communication

Real-time communication is the exchange of information that happens instantly or with minimal delay. In the case of virtual teams, it means communication that occurs immediately or without significant time gaps.

Recommendation Engines

Recommendation engines are AI-powered systems that provide personalized suggestions or recommendations to users based on their preferences and behaviors.

Reputable Websites and Platforms

Reputable Websites and Platforms are online platforms or websites that have a good reputation and are known for providing reliable and trustworthy services. In the context of hiring virtual assistants, reputable websites and platforms refer to platforms like Guided Outsourcing, Upwork, Fiverr, Freelancer.com, and LinkedIn, where entrepreneurs can find and hire virtual assistants with various skills.

Research

Research means gathering information and data for various purposes, such as market analysis or competitor research. Virtual assistants can conduct research tasks and provide valuable insights to an entrepreneur. Use them often!

Scams

Fraudulent or deceptive activities that aim to trick or deceive individuals for financial gain or other malicious purposes. When they are hiring virtual assistants, entrepreneurs need to be alert for potential scams and verify the authenticity of candidates' portfolios and claims.

Scope

In the context of communication with freelancers, scope is the part of project management that defines the boundaries and parameters of the work to be undertaken. It outlines the specific tasks, objectives, deliverables, and expectations that the freelancer is required to fulfill during the course of the project. A well-defined scope ensures that both the client and the freelancer have a shared understanding of the project's goals, thereby minimizing misunderstandings and potential conflicts. Maintaining a well-defined scope is essential throughout the life cycle of a project. As the project progresses, any changes or deviations from the initial scope should be documented and communicated promptly, allowing both parties to assess the impact and make informed decisions.

Search Engine Optimization (SEO)

SEO is the process of optimizing a website or online content to improve its visibility and ranking in search engine results. It utilizes various techniques to attract organic traffic to a website.

Scheduling

Scheduling is the process of coordinating and arranging appointments, meetings, and events. A virtual assistant can handle scheduling tasks, send out invitations, confirm appointments, and make rescheduling arrangements. BIG time saver here!

Social Media Management
Social media management involves managing and maintaining a business's social media presence. A virtual assistant can handle tasks like scheduling posts, responding to messages, engaging with the audience, and monitoring analytics on social media platforms.

Solopreneur
This is a combination of the words "solo" and "entrepreneur." It refers to an individual who runs a one-person business or operates as a self-employed entrepreneur without employees. Being a solopreneur involves wearing multiple hats, as this enterprising individual is not only the creative force behind the business but also the strategic thinker, decision-maker, marketer, financial manager, and customer service representative, among others. This autonomy grants the solopreneur the freedom to shape their business in alignment with their vision and values, enabling them to pursue their passions and interests, and to outsource at will.

Solosocializing
This term was created by the author, Dr. Dorine Rivers, PhD, PMP. It refers to the act of going to a crowded place, such as a coffee shop, with the intention of being alone and not engaging with others present. It is a beautiful balance between getting your solo work done and having a sense of the presence of others: a nice alternative to feeling constantly alone in your office.

Straitjacket
A straitjacket is a garment made of strong material designed to restrain a person's arms and torso tightly. It is used as a means of physical restraint, typically in psychiatric settings.

Symbiotic Relationship

A symbiotic relationship is a mutually beneficial relationship between two or more parties. In the context of this book, it means the beneficial relationship between an entrepreneur and their freelance workers or VAs.

Tech-savvy

Tech-savvy means being knowledgeable and skilled in using technology and digital tools effectively.

Tidal Bore Rafting

Tidal bore rafting means riding the waves created by the incoming tides in certain river estuaries. It is an adventurous water activity in which participants use rafts or kayaks to navigate the powerful tidal currents.

Time Management

The process of planning and organizing tasks and activities to use time effectively and efficiently. It helps entrepreneurs prioritize tasks and allocate time appropriately to maximize productivity.

Tip

In this context, a tip means an additional payment or gratuity given to the virtual assistant as a token of appreciation for excellent work.

Trans-Siberian Railway

The Trans-Siberian Railway is a network of railways that spans Russia, connecting Moscow in the west to Vladivostok in the east. It is one of the longest railways in the world, covering a vast distance.

Trial Work Period

A trial work period is a period during which a candidate is given an opportunity to work on a specific task or project to demonstrate their skills and suitability for the job. Entrepreneurs can ask potential virtual assistants to complete trial tasks before making a final hiring decision.

Value Added Tax (VAT)
Value Added Tax is a consumption tax assessed on the value added to goods and services at each stage of production or distribution. It is used in many countries, including the European Union.

Vetting Process
The vetting process means evaluating and assessing the qualifications, skills, and experience of potential candidates to ensure they meet the required standards and are suitable for the job.

Virtual Assistant (VA)
A virtual assistant is a remote worker who provides administrative, technical, or creative support to businesses and entrepreneurs. They typically work from their own location and communicate with their clients online.

Virtual Team
A virtual team is a group of individuals who collaborate and work together on projects and tasks, but they are not physically located in the same place. Instead, they communicate and collaborate using digital tools and technology.

Website Design
Creating and designing the layout, appearance, and user interface of a website.

Work-Life Balance
Work-life balance refers to the equilibrium between work-related activities and personal life or leisure activities. It means managing time and energy effectively to maintain a healthy lifestyle.

Workflow

The sequence of steps or tasks involved in completing a specific project or process.

Zeal

Great enthusiasm, passion, or eagerness in pursuing a goal or interest.

About the Author

Dorine Rivers, "River" to her friends, literally grew up on North and South American rivers rafting wild whitewater rapids, basking in the sun, and sleeping under a canopy of brilliant constellations. She transferred by osmosis her enthusiasm for the outdoors to her five children (all successful in their own right now) and her twenty grandchildren.

River has an undergraduate degree in creative writing, a Ph.D. in Business Management, Investment Banking and General Contractor licenses, and a few other degrees and certifications in between. She is the CEO of Alpha 81 Inc., an Arizona-based firm successfully supporting corporate innovations, expansions, and exits in software, technology, medical, life/health sciences, education, and other industries.

Her expertise is in strategic planning and management and in building effective business infrastructures by creating and identifying growth opportunities and providing advisory services.

Her award-winning writing, photography, and graphic design have been published in books, magazines, newspapers, brochures, and advertisements. She is also a screenwriter and producer, as well as a developer of online educational courses.

She loves cooking, adventure, and photography, and is an avid biker, hiker, and water sports lover.

Her everyday motto for living is based on Helen Keller's quote:
"Life is either a daring adventure or nothing."

BRAIN TO BANK

HOW TO GET YOUR IDEA OUT OF YOUR HEAD AND CASH IN

Author: Dorine Rivers PhD, PMP
Genre: Non-Fiction / Business & Money
ISBN: 978-0972832205 (Hardback)
ISBN: 978-0972832243 (Paperback)
ISBN: 978-0972832236 (eBook)
Also available in audiobook

BRAIN TO BANK

No matter how brilliant you know your idea to be, the chain of events that brings that idea to market must follow a well-thought-out course of action.

Recognizing and developing well-targeted, innovative products and solutions and launching them on schedule and within budget is complicated.

Brain to Bank is the all-inclusive critical blueprint needed to successfully set in motion your new company, product, or service and help you get your idea out of your head and into the hands of consumers.

As you implement strategic actions to keep driving your idea forward, you'll finally experience your incredible idea going from mind to money.

Brain to Bank fills in the gaps of what you know, what you don't know, and, most importantly, what you don't know you don't know so you can finally cross the finish line and cash in!

Brain to Bank is for the gutsy entrepreneur willing to make it happen!

FREE RESOURCES

I have a plethora of resources and tools that will help you get your idea from brain to bank. I am forever searching for the latest and greatest roadmaps, websites, templates, checklists, guides, and strategies that will make it possible for you to create, market, and sell your product or service. With these additional resources, you'll be able to improve and accelerate getting your idea out of your head and cash in even quicker. Some of these resources include: The complete resources mentioned in the book, including links • Downloadable product development roadmaps, including one for FDA products • A comprehensive project management template • Business plan checklist • Customer avatar template • Distributor avatar template • Outsourcing guides and links • Survey guides and links • And much more. To download these free resources, scan the QR code or go to www.BrainToBank.com/Resources.